BOOK 4
Short -o

Top Job, Bullseye!

978-1-338-57287-2

10 9 8 7 6 5 4 3 2 1   19 20 21 22 23

Printed in Malaysia   106

First printing, 2019

Book design by Marissa Asuncion

Scholastic Inc.

One day, Bullseye found
a little egg.
He did **not** see the **mom**.
Now it was his **job**
to take care of the egg.

His friends did **not** know
if Bullseye was
good for the **job**.
He might **drop** the egg.
He might step **on** it.

But Bullseye did **not** **drop** the egg.
He did **not** step **on** it.
He did a **top job**.

One day
a chick **popped** out!

The chick **hopped on** Bullseye's head. The horse and the chick **got** to be best friends.

The chick learned a **lot** from Bullseye.
He learned to **hop** like a **bronco**.
He learned to **trot** like a horse.

Nothing could **stop** the two friends!

One day, Bullseye saw
a mother hen with some chicks.
The chicks looked like his pal.
Was the hen his pal's
real **mom**?
Yes!

The chick grew into
a fine rooster.
"Bullseye, you did
a **top job** with that chick!"
said Woody.